YOU

& Our Father

Becoming Like a Little Child

JD Nardone

Presence Driven™

This book is dedicated to my oldest son who was declared a "miracle baby", by the hospital staff and doctors, after he was delivered and found to be perfect in every way.

God has used you, Johnny, to change my life in so many ways, but the most significant change was in my relationship with God, as my Dad. Without you, this book could not have been written.

I thank Him for you more often than you know. I'm very proud of you! It warms my heart to be called your Papa.

CONTENTS

The Presence Driven™ Lifestyle is not about having come to the Lord. It is about coming to the Lord on a daily basis, sitting at Jesus' feet, in the Presence of our heavenly Father and becoming like a little child in faith and obedience, so we can access our royal inheritance today and in eternity.

This lifestyle focuses on the eternal instead of the temporal, so you can fix your sight on the future, while preparing for it, in the present. Your ability to see your destiny will keep you from being overwhelmed by current circumstances in your life. We concentrate on the spirit man (new heart) rather than on the natural man (mind). The Presence Driven™ Lifestyle is all about a one-on-one relationship with Papa God through Jesus, instead of a religious, superficial existence with little relevance in everyday life. You develop a lifestyle of seeking and acknowledging His Presence, so His Glory permeates all aspects of your daily life. Each day offers us another opportunity to develop a greater sensitivity to the Holy Spirit, so that we can obey His instructions in every situation and be blessed as literal children of the King.

I find myself wondering if living the Christian life has become too complicated for most of us. As a Christian, have you ever struggled with programs or steps only to fall short and become discouraged? Many have discovered that modern life, with its hectic schedule, is just not compatible with the requirements of a structured program. Please, don't get me wrong. I do believe that programs are beneficial in certain situations, but they are limited over the long-term. We see this shift from program to lifestyle in the area of health/physical fitness. Developing a healthy lifestyle is now promoted over following a diet program, which isn't sustainable over a lifetime. Great things will happen as you begin to develop a lifestyle of speaking to our Dad and hearing from Him. If you are like most of us, then you really do want to hear God's voice and be directed by the Holy Spirit, but with all of the noise (i.e. smart phones/devices, social media, Internet news and entertainment, texting/e-mail, etc.) you can barely hear your own voice, never mind Papa's.

You can learn to hear the still, small voice of the Lord, even in the midst of the whirlwinds of life!

What is a Presence Driven™ Lifestyle? To define Presence Driven™, we must understand the varied meanings of "driven". The Presence Driven™ Lifestyle implies being *driven to* His Presence, by an ever-deepening desire to know your heavenly Father more intimately and receive all the benefits of being a child of God, including spiritual, physical, and financial endowment. In addition, you become *driven by* His Presence, in forward moving progress, as you allow Dad to take control and steer your life according to His perfect plan/vision. Finally, a gentle, yet powerful force will cause you to be *driven away* from the negative, counter-productive aspects of life and the many temptations meant to derail your journey. As we become more like little children in His Presence, we become more and more dependent upon Him for everything including love, affirmation, hope, guidance, encouragement, provision, and a clear vision of our individual assignment (purpose) and destiny. The only way to understand who we are and who we are to become is to spend each day in our heavenly Father's Presence, so we can learn of His ways, see from His point of view, and become Inheritance-Minded™.

Simply, the Presence Driven™ Lifestyle is not about following a formatted program or numbered steps during a prescribed period of time. It is about introducing a few simple things into your life, today, that will enable you to experience a more intimate relationship with God, recognize His voice more often throughout the day, and live in His will and provision more fully.

Introduction

It seems that a majority of Christians struggle to truly identify with their "new *identity* in Christ". Many do not feel the *security* that a member of the Royal Family of God should experience—regardless of life's issues and circumstances.[1] Others struggle to understand that God's *acceptance* has little to do with what *we* do or do not do, so they are often unsure of how God views them, on a daily basis.[2] Additionally, it's obvious that everyone is searching for her/his personal *assignment* (purpose/meaning of his/her individual life). One cannot have these "four core needs of the heart" satisfied by simply reading the Bible to find the general purposes for life, and then striving to do the things that he/she feels will fulfill these needs. If I, as a child of God, am going to discover why God created *me* with a unique combination of natural skills/abilities, life experiences, and spiritual gifts, then I must spend time in the Presence of the only One who can answer this question—the only One who can provide the resources to succeed.[3] Our Father God is the only One who can give us our "new identity", make us feel secure and accepted, and reveal our individual assignment—our destiny!

Have you noticed that many contemporary approaches to living the "Christian" life have become quite complicated? Have you ever wondered why becoming a child of God is as easy as confessing with our mouths and believing in our hearts, but then it seems rather difficult to live-out our lives with eternal significance?[4] Why would our loving, merciful, and good Father make it so complicated? It doesn't make sense, right? Living as a Follower of Jesus, a child of God should be simple, too! Of course, at times it may not be easy, but that's just life. Our relationship with our Dad should be simple, period!

I encourage you to read on and discover that Jesus taught a simple approach to living and experiencing a life overflowing with love, peace, hope, and provision. Jesus didn't teach programs, steps, or complicated requirements, but He did say, "...you are worried and troubled about many things. ***But one thing is needed***", so "***do not worry or be anxious about tomorrow***, for tomorrow will have worries and anxieties of its own."[5]

Isn't it a relief to know that there is only one thing necessary and if we simply focus on that one thing, today, we can experience all of the promises of God and enjoy Full-Life™ Wealth?

Maybe, it really is as simple as becoming like a little child and investing time in our Father's Presence.

Chapter One

My Three Year Old Son

"Then they brought little children to Him, that He might touch them; but the disciples rebuked those who brought them. But when Jesus saw [it], He was indignant and pained and said to them, Allow the children to come to Me—do not forbid or prevent or hinder them—for to such belongs the kingdom of God. **Truly, I tell you, whoever does not receive and accept and welcome the kingdom of God like a little child [does] positively shall not enter it at all.** And He took them [the children up one by one] in His arms and [fervently invoked a] blessing, placing His hands upon them."[1]

One - My Three Year Old Son

During one of my extended prayer times, in preparation for writing this book, I heard the Lord say, "Your son is Presence Driven." The next day I began the process of observing my son's behavior, so I could document how a little child lives out their day—prioritizing time and engaging Papa. What I discovered has changed my life and the lives of many others who have already begun living a Presence Driven Lifestyle, by becoming like little children.[2]

We understand that three and four year olds are little children, so to become like little children we must understand their attributes and learn how they view life and respond to authority.[3] As I began studying my three year old son, I started recognizing that little children are wholly, Presence Driven. His daily existence is driven to and by the presence of his Papa.

Fatherless

I want to clarify my personal perspective, so that we can proceed on stable ground. First, I was raised by a single mother in the '60s/'70s and at that time it was not chic, socially acceptable, or a choice that was considered desirable, as it seems to be in our society, today. I knew who my father was, but did not know anything about him and never spoke to him until I was almost fourteen years old. Obviously, I understand that a single mother often has to perform the roles of both mother and father, but for the purpose of this book and based on my personal experience with my son, I will use "Papa" when referring to the parent, authority figure, or guardian in a little child's life. Second, I am not a perfect father by a long shot and I never had a role model parent growing-up, so I have had to rely on the Bible, prayer, and my deep desire to be the loving, affirming father that I never had, but always longed to have in my life. Sure, it was difficult for me to relate to God as my Father, in the beginning of my relationship with Him, but I chose to accept Him as my perfect Dad. I was determined to spend much time seeking Him through prayer and learning about His character by reading the Old Testament. Of course, after I became a father, my perspective and understanding changed, which only served to deepen my relationship with our Father. I often find myself contemplating just how much He loves me, when reflecting on how much I love my sons.

I believe that one of the primary reasons why people have a difficult time relating to God as Father is because many of us never had a father in the home. And for others who did have a father that was present in the home, their experience may not have been one based on unconditional love, compassion, understanding, communication, and discipline, all balanced in a Biblical way. Often times, a father spends little time in the home due to work. For those of you who did grow up with a father, who used the Bible as a guide for their role, much of this book will be familiar, but for those of us who did not grow up with a father who modeled God's character and applied Biblical principles in their role as head of the family, it should be particularly insightful. Now, that you have a glimpse into my life and personal viewpoint, let me introduce you to my son's.

A Day in the Life of a Little Child

The first thing that my son does when he wakes-up is call, "Papa" because he desires and seeks my presence. In the case of my son, he doesn't wait long before he calls, "Papa", again. If I do not come right away, he'll make a move because he is actively pursuing his heart's desire—to be in my presence. He finds his way into my bedroom. To be in Papa's presence is what he "needs", first thing in the morning, so he comes closer and calls, "Papa", announcing himself and implying his intentions. When he comes closer and says, "Papa", he is letting me know that he is taking steps to come closer into my presence, but that is not enough for him. He desires more, yes, he needs contact, so the little child climbs into Papa's bed, pressing into my presence. He crawls close enough to place his face next to mine and whispers, "Papa, are you awake?" You see he is actively seeking Papa's presence, which to him is a closeness, an embrace, a tangible confirmation that acknowledges his pursuit of me. He is not discouraged if my answer does not come quickly. He *needs* me to communicate with him and acknowledge that he has moved closer, so he keeps repeating, "Papa, are you awake?" I may be asleep or may just remain silent, but my son is not deterred from his heartfelt goal. He simply continues asking until I say, "Good morning, Son."

Immediately, he invites me to come with him and join in his life, which is simple and now—in the present! My son humbly acknowledges his need for me by asking me to help him get his day started. He asks me to meet his "needs" throughout the day, whether to eat, go potty, play, read a book, anything, and everything. This little child simply understands that all the provision he needs is supplied in my presence. Papa is his provider, teacher, helper, supporter, strength, advocate, and even healer, when I make his "boo-boo" better, so he doesn't look anywhere else. He acknowledges my authority and submits to it, willingly, because he has learned that the results of obedience, including Papa's blessing, protection, and provision, are better than the consequences of disobedience. My little son has already learned to sow seeds of obedience and submission, so he reaps the resulting harvest of blessing.

Good Morning!

After I say, "good morning, Son" he will lay with me and cuddle and just rest and wait in my presence, close to me, looking into my face, whether my eyes are open or not. Finally, my son asks, "Papa, what do you want to do?" I often wonder just how many of us, professing Christians, get this basic principle right. It is easier for us to "save time" by jumping to the point of our own needs and desires and then ending the conversation by darting off to engage our day. I hope that I am not the only one who falls into this "trap of life", which only leads to prayers that lack power and frustration born of uncertainty about our true relationship with Father God.

The little one continues, "Do you want to get-up, do you want to play, do you want to read, do you want to eat, do you want to go?" I eventually communicate exactly what I want to do and he never argues, debates, or tries to make me reconsider or change my mind. He just says, "Let's go, Papa!" This is exactly what we are supposed to do each morning, as God's little children.

At other times, I will simply begin a dialogue with my son by saying, "No, Papa's tired." He will respond by sharing his desires. My son may say, "Come" and I say, "Where?" He'll continue, "With me" and I reply, "Why?" He declares, "I want milk, I want you to play with me, I want to show you."

After we communicate for a while, he grabs my hand tightly and starts pulling, as he urges, "Papa, come with me, help me, feed me, play with me!" He has determined in his heart that he is not going to do anything outside of my presence, even though he has many desires and few "needs", his primary *need* is to be in Papa's presence today. Can you honestly say that in this sense you have become like a little child?

As a loving father, who recognizes my son's deep desire and persistent attitude, I must respond to his *need* by joining him and contributing to his day. This little child began by seeking and requesting his Papa's presence and intimate contact, as a necessity and without yielding, so that is what he receives.

Face-to-Face

Now that we are "connected", we begin moving ahead with the day's activities. My son is not satisfied, though, with simply holding my hand and walking next to me in his own power and ability. No, he entreats "Up!" This little child positions himself right in front of Papa, so I have to stop and look down at him. As I am forced, by his persistence, to stop and turn my attention to him, what do I see? I see a little boy with a big smile, whose eyes are filled with the expectation of what he will see when he is lifted up, face-to-face with Papa. In addition, both of his arms are reaching up in acknowledgment that I am higher and he needs me to lift him up to my higher perspective. I see my son standing on his tiptoes and fully extending his reach, as he does everything in his power to get "Up". His actions have become so animated that it's easy for me to recognize that his desire to see more has become an urgent "need". He begins to cry-out, "Papa up, Papa up, Papa up!"

What can a loving father do? There is no time for excuses or preoccupation on my part. He has given me no other choice, but to respond immediately to his need. My son *needs* to see the world from my perspective. His desire to see as Papa sees has transformed into a *need*, which he is expressing through his actions, not just his words. My son, whom I love, has positioned himself at my feet, his eyes, arms, and voice lifted with urgency, leaving me with a simple decision. I *must* pick him up, elevate him, and exalt him above his condition and limitations, so he can have his *need* fulfilled. Now, he begins to see from my viewpoint, which is high above his natural position as a little child.

How often do we lift up our hands to our heavenly Father as a declaration that we want "Up"? Many of us are too proud or embarrassed to become like little children in the Presence of the Lord, but if you want to see from His perspective, then you must act like a little child and humbly position yourself to be lifted up.[4]

Finally! We are now face-to-face and I can whisper in my little one's ear with a soft, gentle tone because we are so close. He is listening as we are looking at life, situations, and circumstances from the same perspective. I don't have to speak loudly to be heard because we are face-to-face. I can be sure that he is paying attention to every word because we are eye-to-eye. I can give him a gentle kiss to show him my affection because we are cheek-to-cheek. We are face-to-face, so I am assured that he sees exactly what I see from my point of view. As we walk past the mirror and stop to observe the reflection of our two faces next to each other, I can see in his eyes and his smile that he is beginning to perceive and understand that I am his Papa and we are alike. In our closeness, he experiences my superior strength, loving embrace, and desire to take him places he cannot go without me. He is beginning to appear more like his Papa and perceive life from my vantage point, so he sees things that he was unable to see from his subordinate position. I can see in his facial expressions that he feels this is a good position for him, a natural place.

"No, Up!"

As we move forward my son begins to slip down a bit due to the effect of activity and external pressures, but he doesn't want to lose his face-to-face perspective. Just as he recognizes that his face is no longer next to mine, but at chest level, he begins to squirm and climb back up to his desired position—face-to-face. Simultaneously, he begins to say, "No, up, up!" with an urgent tone because he *needs* to get higher. He is taking affirmative action to ensure he stays, "Up!" This little child simply cannot accept a lower perspective, if even for a moment. He knows that I still have him firmly in my grasp, he is safe, he is secure, I love him, and he is in my presence, but he desires, as a vital necessity, all that I can offer him. He wants to be face-to-face with Papa in an intimate, transcendent position, which provides the supreme viewpoint.[5] This higher perspective enables him to see more of the environment, understand circumstances more competently, and hear each whispered instruction, accurately. He is abiding in Papa's presence, face-to-face, and nothing is more satisfying. As we see life and communicate from this shared perspective, we are bonding and my son is "finding" *his* identity in me.

I have experienced this in my own life with our Father God. One day I feel that I'm face-to-face, seeing everything from His higher perspective and obstacles seem so small, but then "life" takes over and before I know it, I have allowed myself to slip down to a lower perspective. I've adjusted to it without a struggle and all of life's issues seem so much bigger. This may have happened to you, too. Many of us reach-out to our heavenly Father and He lifts us up to enable us to see our situation from His point of view, but then life begins to place demands and burdens upon us, pulling us down. It can happen so subtly that we may not notice the change in our position, our perspective, right away. Suddenly, the day comes when we are faced with a dramatic change or challenge in our circumstances and we can only see the situation from our natural, lower point of view. Often, we struggle and strive to 'figure out' why things have changed and what we should do to stabilize our situation. Eventually, we realize that we don't have all the answers and we are not supposed to handle everything on our own, so we run to Papa, as little children. If you want to see your "world", as God sees it, then you must develop a Presence Driven Lifestyle.

Chapter Two

Attributes of Little Children

"Therefore, whoever humbles himself like this child
is the greatest in the kingdom"[1]

Two - Attributes of Little Children

What does it mean to become like a little child? Well, if you are like those of us who seem to have an insatiable drive to overachieve, characterized by setting excessive performance standards or if you live with low self-esteem and/or rejection on multiple levels, then it means taking the greatest risk of all. Becoming child-like requires us to trust God, our heavenly Father, with absolutely everything in our lives, whether large or small. It is the pinnacle of faith to trust Him with *all* of our accomplishments and status, dreams and plans for the future, and material and intangible wealth. At the same time, this decision is the true beginning of our spiritual maturity and the foundation of our ongoing relationship with God as Father. The truth is that for an adult it may seem like a great risk, but for a little child it is simply, life.

Little children are not "in control" of their lives. The primary issue is that most of us are taught, from a young age, that being self-reliant and "in control" is synonymous with "growing-up" and adulthood. We strive to plan our future, control our present, and influence outcomes. All of our planning, control, and influence serves to feed our egos, help us establish self-worth, and support the perception (of power and authority) that we have of ourselves and others have of us. Little children do not worry about tomorrow; they simply live in the present.[2] They remain focused on today, which enables them to "experience" everything. A little child does not have cares and burdens because they know that whatever they need will be supplied by Papa/Mama. They

24

simply ask, expecting to receive, and they continue asking and asking until they have what they desire.[3]

Little children have not been influenced by information, opinions, self-determined purpose, and worldly perceptions of relative truths and success. They believe what they hear and are always listening. There are times when a parent may think that their little one is not hearing, but listening to the child speak and ask questions, reveals that they have indeed heard everything! They typically don't waste time analyzing or debating, but simply obey instructions and yield to authority. Our heavenly Father is simple too, because He is God who created the heavens and earth with His words, so *everything* is simple for Him. God is simple because nothing is complex, worrisome, or beyond just a word. You see, He created the earth with just a word and nothing is impossible with God.[4]

We, in our hyper-analytical, incessant problem solving, information-overloaded adult lives struggle to simply trust our Father and allow Him to "handle" everything. Most adults and even many teenagers have been tainted by the world's system and influenced by its standards of success. We are literally, petrified by the abundance of information that we consume on a daily basis and apathy has become a widely accepted norm. The rich young ruler, in the Bible, was told to become like a little child, but he chose to hold on to life as he knew it, with title/position, money, and influence, rather than follow Jesus and become who he was really created to be, as a child of God.[5] By the world's standards he was wealthy, but by the kingdom of God's standard and within his own heart he was poor and lacking.[6] You must be born-again *and* become like a little child if you want to see yourself as God created you and truly believe in your divine destiny.

To experience Full-Life Wealth, we must leave the world's system behind and actively live according to God's kingdom system, each day. Most of us do not recognize our Father's intervention in our lives, so we take Him for granted. We miss multiple opportunities each day, to acknowledge Him and learn from Him. Little children, on the other hand, are always being amazed because they are always looking to discover something, whether great or small. An ever-increasing worship is a direct result of an ever-increasing amazement with the love and provision of the Father whose mercy is new every morning.[7]

You were intelligently created to be unique. You have been filled with all of the spiritual seeds of greatness needed and equipped with natural skills and abilities, then refined by all of your individual life experiences to be the greatest "you".[8] You were not created to be a better version of someone else. We cannot "live-out" our divine assignment and reach our destiny by comparing ourselves to others and setting benchmarks based on what others do, say, or achieve. You and I can only achieve eternal success when we are living in our Father's will and walking on the path that He has prepared for each of us, individually.

Little children live a Presence Driven Lifestyle, one day at a time, totally dependent on an "adult" who has sovereign authority over everything. You are supposed to submit your entire life to our

Father's sovereign authority, as His little child. Isn't it interesting that after years of conditioning as grown-ups, we are told by self-help gurus to be introspective, so we can rediscover the child within, thereby identifying our "real" selves and unleashing the sleeping giant?

As I continued to observe my first-born, five distinct attributes became obvious. I must clarify that we never experienced the "terrible twos" and my wife and I give all the glory to God for this blessing. If you have children and some of the following attributes were absent or scarce in your 3-4 year old, please realize that these are the "ideal" attributes, which our Father expects us to model, as His little children. If you are a parent, then I am sure that you, too, will find these attributes to be highly desirable! Please, as you read, reflect on your life to determine if these beneficial attributes are on display in *your* personal relationship with God.

Submitted to Established Authority

First, little children are **submissive** in relation to the "authority" figure in their lives. They are able to submit to the will of the "one" above. The Bible tells that Jesus understood this fact and submitted His will to the Father's, "Then He (Jesus) said to them, My soul is very sad and deeply grieved, so that I am almost dying of sorrow. Stay here and keep awake and keep watch with Me. And going a little farther, He threw Himself upon the ground on His face and prayed saying, My Father, if it is possible, let this cup pass away from Me; nevertheless, not what I will [not what I desire], but as You will and desire."[9] After He

27

submitted His desire, to our Father, Jesus was positioned to be "obedient to the point of death...Therefore God also has highly exalted Him and gave Him the name which is above every name"[10] We all must pray, "Our Father in heaven...Your kingdom come, Your will be done in my life", if we desire to live as His little children.[11]

Obedient to Specific Instructions

Second, they are *obedient* and eager to follow direct instructions and receive wise guidance. Little children want to learn and succeed in life, so they are teachable. They don't yet know enough to "know it all" in their own minds, so they are obedient without analyzing, debating, or doubting. The more they obey, the more they realize they don't really know anything without instruction from above. Each of us must learn to recognize the voice of our heavenly Father, so that we can obey His specific instructions, each day. No one can complete their assignment and reach their destiny without His direction, wisdom, and protection.

There is no other "seed" required to live in the blessing of your heavenly Father. Your *giving* of money, time, talents, etc. is simply a result of obedience.[12] We don't own a thing. We are just stewards of His provision. You may ask, "What then, JD? If I don't feel comfortable or am unwilling to give money, time, talents, etc., am I living in disobedience?" My answer to you, dear reader, is simply and unequivocally, "Yes." Don't stop reading now or close your heart, but press on towards your untapped potential as Father God's little child and you will never be the same. I promise!

Humble and Forgiving

Third, little children are forgiving, which is a byproduct of their inherent ***humility***, which is reinforced by time spent in our Father's Presence. It is impossible to be forgiving without humility. Humility is defined as lowliness, meekness, lack of false pride, perseverance, modest opinion or estimate of one's own importance, and forgiving, which certainly describes little children.[13] These are the same conditions of the heart that Jesus exhorted us to have, if we are to access the kingdom of God and our royal inheritance here on earth.[14] I believe that one of the most prevalent hindrances to God's blessing is unforgiveness, which is a result of pride. As a matter of fact, it has been reported that many physical and mental illnesses are rooted in unforgiveness. It is a cancer that eventually contaminates the heart and overwhelms the mind. Forgiveness opens the doors to relationships because all of us need to be forgiven.

After I discipline my son and he is finished crying, he isn't held back from my presence and blessing because of unforgiveness on my part. He comes to me and we continue with our loving relationship. One day my son came home from school and mentioned that a classmate said something mean to him, and then the very next day, he came to tell me about how much fun he had playing with the same classmate! I pray, "Father God, help us to be forgiving, as you are forgiving towards us and help us to remember that we need your mercy each day. In

29

Jesus Name, Amen." In this way, may we all become like little children.

You may be thinking, "JD, I always forgive and hold no resentment." My question to you is, "Do you rely on God for everything?" Is there anything in your life that you feel qualified to handle on your own, like brushing your teeth or getting to work on time? You may find it silly for me to speak of brushing teeth, but when I began asking God to help me with little things; it became much easier to confess my dependence on Him for everything in my life. Pride can be subtle and deceiving, yet it will lead to resentment and unforgiveness. In our Father's Presence, there is no room for pride or unforgiveness. The reality of our utter dependence on Him and the depth of His mercy can only be revealed in His Presence. No one can sit in Father God's Presence without being overwhelmed by His love, forgiveness, and power. Live a Presence Driven Lifestyle and you will experience this Truth!

Letting Love Rule

Fourth, little children love, unconditionally, because they have pure hearts. Their hearts have not been tainted by pride, resentment, and/or unforgiveness. My son loves freely because he is loved freely and in Papa's presence, he finds continuous love. He is filled with love, so he has much love to give to others. One of the greatest compliments that my wife and I ever received was from our son's teachers in his PK class. On different occasions, different teachers told us that he looked and acted loved. Now, I am not sure how they

30

"qualified" their observations, but I do know that they were accurate. We made a concerted effort to "make" him feel loved from birth, and the result had an impact on other people! When you live a Presence Driven Lifestyle, you experience Love every day. You'll feel loved and others will feel it, too!

Persistent and Influential

Finally, they exhibit the vital trait of *persistence*, which is invaluable in any stage of life. My son is determined to receive my best, so he is persistent in his pursuit. He is convinced in his heart that I want to bless him, so he repeats his petition over and over and over. If you have raised children or have little children, then you know what I mean. They just don't give up! Many of us fall into the trap of praying for something a few times and then get distracted by "life".[15] We either forget to continue our petitioning or simply give-up. I encourage you to be like a little child in the Presence of our Father and "Keep on asking and it will be given you; keep on seeking and you will find; keep on knocking [reverently] and [the door] will be opened to you."[16]

Chapter Three

Living Everyday as a Little Child

"I tell you the truth, unless you change and become like little children, you will never enter the kingdom"[1]

"At that time Jesus, full of joy through the Holy Spirit, said, "I praise you, Father, Lord of heaven and earth, because you have hidden these things from the wise and learned, and revealed them to little children. Yes, Father, for this was your good pleasure."[2]

Three – Living Everyday as a Little Child

Believing Like a Little Child

What I love most about Jesus' teachings is that he brought the kingdom of God to us, where we are, and translated kingdom principles into simple, yet profound, parables and statements. His instructions can be understood by all of us regardless of education, background, language, or geographic location. He, masterfully, focused His teachings on making the incomprehensible, simple to access. Jesus gave us Truths/keys, which He expressed in a variety of ways, making them understandable and executable at our level. In fact, He simplified everything down to two commandments or instructions that even a little child can not only understand, but can also accomplish each and every day.[3]

Little children live Presence Driven, one day at a time, not worrying about life's needs.[4] They look to Papa for all of their provision and are confident that he is enough. We must become like little children by sitting at Jesus' feet, in our heavenly Father's Presence, today.[5] Living a Presence Driven Lifestyle means relying on and trusting in our Father to provide for all of our spiritual, physical, and financial needs and desires, whether large or small. The Presence Driven Lifestyle is characterized by totally trusting, obeying, and submitting in *all* areas of your life, every day.

Every Desire is a "Need"

When my son says, "I want..." and does not get what he requests right away or he receives an answer that he is not satisfied with, he quickly communicates his desire as a *need*. He replaces "I want..." with "I need..." and with amazing persistence he continues to petition with a new level of urgency in his tone! A little child believes with all his heart, that Papa has all the answers. In the eyes of my son, Papa can do anything and provide everything, so he is motivated to keep asking until he gets what he desires or "needs".

We begin our lives by pursuing each desire with passion and persistence because, as little children, we commit wholeheartedly to what we perceive as a need. Little children are highly resistant to yielding or giving up their requests because of this passionate pursuit of every "need". As adults, maybe we become too analytical and say, "That would be nice, *but* I better live in the *real* world." Do we think this way, so we won't get disappointed, again? Has life in the "real" world thrown you some unexpected curves, causing you to give-up or postpone your dreams or heartfelt desires? Little children don't, I mean won't give-up on their dreams. They just keep dreaming bigger and bigger as new possibilities are revealed. Their imagination continues to develop in the presence of their "almighty", "wonder working" Papa. God wants us to keep dreaming bigger dreams, as we experience His boundless power, provision, and love in His Presence. "For with God nothing is ever impossible and no word from God shall be without power or impossible of fulfillment."[6] Are you ready to rekindle the "dreams of your youth" and trust our Papa God for the "impossible"? Are you ready to dream new dreams, "impossible" dreams?

Hiding from Papa

Avoiding Papa's presence does happen when the little one knows that his disobedience is uncovered and chastening will be administered. Adam and Eve hid from Abba because they knew that they had disobeyed His instructions.[7] They understood that they were now exposed and deserving of disciplinary action.[8] Guilt produces insecurity and running or "hiding" from Papa only compounds the guilt and feeds apprehension. The greater the time between sin and repentance, the greater the anxiety we have about Fatherly correction, forgiveness, and reconciliation. Doesn't the delay just make us feel worse? Of course, we may not know the specific consequences, but we know that "God's mercy is new each morning" and "He is love", so even His chastening is done with mercy and followed-up with unconditional love.[9]

This is a perfect model for parents and one that I regularly work to emulate. When I have a conversation with my son and the topic is disobedience (i.e. rebellion against authority, *the root of sin*), I always end with a hug, loving embrace, and kiss.[10] I want to be sure that my little child understands that I love him very much, unconditionally. He has to learn that it is because I love him, that I cannot tolerate his willful disobedience. Submission to authority facilitates his protection! All I ask of him is that he obeys. He already understands that it is not "him" that displeases me, but his act of disobedience.

After he has had his time-out or has cried himself through, in his room, he never fails to come over to me with an expression of repentance, love, and thankfulness for the loving correction. Really! This is one of the most fascinating and instructive areas of our father/son relationship. My little child understands that Papa loves him and this is why I must help him do the right thing, to obey. He recognizes that even though I do not approve of his behavior I still love him very much, care for him, and want him to be in my presence. I don't bring up his actions again. I simply embrace him and quickly move to honor his desire to be reconciled and blessed. As God's children, we should follow this example and run to our Father, thanking Him that He loves us enough to chasten us.[11] Is this how you respond to our Father's love?

Parenting and Discipline

I remember when our first child was born and my wife and I discussed discipline. She seemed to think that my idea of complete obedience, in action and timing, was a bit too much, so we read all of the Bible verses about rearing children and reviewed the consequences of disobedience. She became more agreeable, but honestly, I could tell that she would be content to leave this area of rearing to me. That was until I gave her the following examples, which illustrated the necessity of absolute obedience in our son. She soon realized that we cannot protect our little child from immediate, life altering danger unless he learns to obey. Our Father wants to protect us, too, but first we must learn to recognize His Voice!

I asked her, "What will happen when our son begins to walk and he slips by your grasp, headed towards a hot oven, and you call-out with a tone and volume of urgency, "Son, no, stop!", but he disobeys and touches the glowing oven"? At this point, her facial expression changed, and so did her attitude towards teaching our son obedience and submission to authority. I continued, "And what would happen if the two of you are walking in our driveway and he decides to take off running into the street, without noticing an oncoming car and you voice the command, "Stop!", but he decides not to obey and keeps running?" These two realistic scenarios helped her recognize that teaching our son obedience was not an option, but our obligation as loving parents.

We understand then, why our heavenly Father requires us to simply obey His commands and submit to His authority. The Bible says that "Obedience is better than sacrifice, and submission is better than (an) offering".[12] Jesus stated, "if you love me you will keep my commands".[13] We are also warned not to "despise chastening because our Father only chastens those He loves".[14] Thank God that He has kept things simple by giving us only two choices: to be obedient and be blessed or disobedient and be cursed.[15]

Many parents, today, fail to follow the Bible's instructions and our Father's example in the rearing of their children.[16] Some parents fail to discipline, so they raise rebellious children. Others discipline, but don't take the time to lovingly instruct because they are too busy, so they produce children who grow-up with low self-esteem, feelings of rejection, and/or deep rooted fear. In the past, the cry of the youth was, "My parents are too strict", but today, the loudest and most prevalent cry is, "My parents don't care". Kids feel abandoned, even though they live with one or both parents, because of a lack of discipline and consistent involvement by parents in their day-to-day lives. Some parents pursue more money to buy more things, but neglect to invest significant time in their most valuable asset, their children. Most kids don't *really* want more "things". They want to feel loved by us, through our giving of more time *and* discipline! Children are a blessing, not a burden. Do you feel like a burden or a blessing to our Father? If you have children, how do you think they feel? How did you feel, as a child growing up?

These scenarios and others explain why it is often very difficult to trust Father God with our one, whole life. We struggle and resist letting go and "letting" God *be* our Father. Many of us may have a distorted understanding of how a loving Father acts, unless we study the Bible to learn the true character of Daddy, our God. Family is the most important priority to God, which is why He gave His only begotten Son.[17] Becoming like a little child, again, may seem like a huge risk, but if you spend time in our heavenly Father's Presence by sitting at Jesus' feet, then you will learn to trust Him and faith will be your guide, instead of fear.

All Grown-Up

Most of us "grow-up" looking forward to the day when we become independent of parental oversight. Moving into "my own place" and "paying my own way" are the benchmarks for becoming an adult. We are encouraged to be independent and "grow-up", so we habitually try to prove that we don't need anyone to provide for our needs. We do this by living self-reliant, self-aware, and self-centered lives, which align with societal standards. I understand the difficulty associated with surrendering this deeply established independence. You see, I was forced to begin working and paying rent at the tender age of fourteen, so my "identity" was rooted in my independence and ability to survive on my own. But, little children are not in control of their lives, do not have "opinions", and have not proven that they can "make it" on their own.

As little children mature, parents encourage them to make decisions about what to wear, what to do, how to spend time, who to be friends with, etc. Typically, we start growing-up and enjoy having more "control" over our lives. We have learned enough to begin making decisions, but are still under the authority of Papa. You may be familiar with the declaration, "If you are going to live under my roof (Presence, protection, provision), then you are going to obey my rules (submit to my authority)" made by the parent who loves his/her children enough to establish and enforce rules and order in their lives. Likewise, our Father wants you to live according to His plan, which is only revealed a few steps at a time, as you live in His Presence, as His little child.

We want to plan everything, but when we confess Jesus as our Savior *and* Lord we are born-again and instructed to become and *act* like little children, wholly dependent on our heavenly Father for everything.[18] Little children understand this! They seek the daily plan from the Chief Planner, Daddy, not so they can debate and analyze, but so they can rest and enjoy the benefits of living a Presence Driven Lifestyle. Jesus said that without Him we can do nothing and "nothing" still means zero.[19]

Chapter Four

Every Child Needs to Know Their Father

"Jesus, **knowing** that the Father had given all things into His hands, and that He had come from God and was going to God, rose from supper and laid aside His garments, took a towel and girded Himself. After that, He poured water into a basin and began to wash the disciples' feet, and to wipe them with the towel with which He was girded."[1]

"He (Jesus) threw Himself upon the ground on His face and prayed saying, My Father, if it is possible, let this cup pass away from Me; **nevertheless, not what I will [not what I desire], but as You will and desire.**"[2]

Four – Every Child Needs to Know Their Father

We must talk about the four core needs of the heart, which include **identity**, **security**, **acceptance**, and **assignment** *(specific, individual purpose)*. Every human perpetually seeks, in varied ways, to have these essential needs quenched, but they can only be fully satisfied in our Father's Presence.

We can't just read about our new "identity" in Christ and/or listen to sermons.[3] You must learn what it really means to be a child of God from Daddy God, Himself. He, alone, can give you your "new" name (who *He* calls you). As you spend more time in His Presence, just the two of you, you'll begin to feel a high level of "security" and "acceptance", which is needed as you pursue your "assignment".

Core Heart Need 1: Identity

"Nor shall your name any longer be Abram [high, exalted father]; but your name shall be Abraham [father of a multitude], for I have made you the father of many nations."[4]

It is only in our heavenly Father's Presence that our "new", royal identity can be revealed to us and confirmed in our hearts. Ponder for a moment what happens in a natural family. We all receive a family name when we are born. Is this the family name of the mother or the father? Obviously, we receive our family name from our father. Of course, we begin to derive our identity from our mother,

44

while we are in the womb and in the very early weeks and months of life. My identity is expanded and clarified, as I grow to become a little child and spend more time in my father's presence. It is this critical phase of growth, which many of us never experience in our families and a majority of Christians never pursue after their initial born-again experience. It is easy to look at "becoming like a little child" as regression, but if you really believe that you *are* born-again, then growing from a newborn into a little child is actually progression and maturing into your new identity.

In other words, your identity is completed in and through your relationship with our Father. When a child grows-up without their father in the home and/or a meaningful, loving relationship with him, there is a "part" missing. No matter how hard a mother tries, she cannot fill or complete this needed "part" of the heart for the little child. Likewise, there is no one who can take the place of Father God, in your life!

Our spiritual, eternal identity can only be provided by our heavenly Father and received in His Presence. Through a daily process of transformation, we begin to reflect Him just like Moses' face reflected His glory after he spent time in God's Presence.[5] We can only reflect Him if we spend time in His Glory/Presence.[6] Most of us associate our "identity" with our profession, position/title, finances, or other external, temporal things. If you "confess with your mouth, Jesus is Lord, and believe in your heart that God raised him from the dead", then your primary identity is "child of God" and all other roles

45

or "identities" must become subordinate.[7] Only our Father can reveal your eternal name, which connects you to your assignment.[8]

Core Heart Need 2: Security

"Have I not commanded you? Be strong and courageous. Do not be afraid; do not be discouraged, for the LORD your God will be with you wherever you go."[9]

True and eternal security can only be provided by our heavenly Father. It is in His Presence that we begin to experience His almighty power. It is in Father God's Presence where we recognize that all we need is a healthy relationship with the omnipotent One. You can read about Him in the Bible and hear the testimonies of others, but until *you* experience His Presence on a daily basis, you can only try to imagine how secure you really are, as His royal child. If we listen to the news each day, it is easy to feel insecure, vulnerable, or worried about the security of our natural family, but if we live a Presence Driven Lifestyle, then we will always feel secure "under the shadow of the Almighty."[10] Regardless of "wars and rumors of wars", terrorist attacks, or the ever-darkening worldview propagated through mass media, you are not to be fearful because "a thousand may fall at your side and ten thousand at your right hand, but it shall not come near you."[11]

Core Heart Need 3: Acceptance

*"When Simon Peter saw it, he fell down at Jesus'
knees, saying, "Depart from me, for I am a sinful
man, O Lord!"...And Jesus said to Simon, "Do not
be afraid. From now on you will catch men.""*[12]

This need of acceptance is a powerful
motivator in our lives and can lead us down many
deceptive and destructive paths in search of
fulfillment. Life sustaining acceptance is found in our
Father's affirmation, which can only be "felt" and
take root in His Presence. Without acceptance, we are
lost in a sea of doubt about our significance.

We understand that teen violence, teen sex,
and sexual immorality are often the result of a
desperate need for acceptance. Teenage boys and girls
join gangs because they "need" to be accepted and
they find it in their gang "family". Teenage girls are
drawn to sex because of this unmet need, often
resulting from the absence of their father in the home.
Drug use produces acceptance among other drug
users. We also see story after story of people engaged
in the homosexual "lifestyle", which is often rooted in
the lack of acceptance from their fathers. This need
may drive a young man to seek acceptance from an
older man, who takes the place of his missing father.
A young woman may seek affection from a woman
because of her distrust of or lack of a healthy
emotional connection with men. This universal need
for acceptance is a powerful driving force in all of us.

Additionally, many people are deceived into
thinking that money and marketplace success will fill

47

this void and quench this need of acceptance. Financial wealth and status among peers and family often lead us away from dependence on our Father. We see so many "successful" people afflicted with the pride of possessions and fear of losing material wealth, which keeps many well-intended souls from their destiny. I've coached a number of extremely successful businesspeople who believed that financial wealth was their destiny, yet, at the same time they felt in their hearts that there must be more to life. As we worked together, most of them discovered, and then admitted that no amount of money could quench this need for acceptance.

Core Heart Need 4: Assignment

"Then Mary took a pound of very costly oil of spikenard, anointed the feet of Jesus, and wiped His feet with her hair...But Jesus said, "Let her alone; she has kept this for the day of My burial. Assuredly, I say to you, wherever this gospel is preached in the whole world, what this woman has done will also be told as a memorial to her.""[13]

We have already discovered that your assignment can only be revealed by the One Who knows why you were created in the first place. If you are tired of living a life driven by the general purposes outlined in other books and have longed to discover your exact and perfect assignment, then you must begin to live a Presence Driven Lifestyle. It is in His Presence that your assignment is revealed and access to your royal inheritance (in other words all of the required provision) is guaranteed!

Only your Creator knows your individual assignment and divine destiny.[14] In recent years, millions of people have been talking about being driven by the general purposes of life that can be found in the written Word of God, but I'm not speaking about those.[15] Our heavenly Father created you to solve a unique problem, engage in a specific assignment, and reach your divinely appointed destiny.[16] Your assignment can only be understood and, even more importantly, accomplished by living a Presence Driven Lifestyle. It has never been God's intention for you to conduct self-assessments or an inventory of your natural skills and gifts, so you can "figure-out" your life assignment. God alone is the Creator, Potter, and Author of your life. He alone can speak to your heart, direct your daily activities, and supply all of the needed provision, so that your success is guaranteed![17]

Where are You Seeking?

Every born-again child of God must become like a little child, living a Presence Driven Lifestyle at the feet of Jesus, in our Father God's Presence, so that these four core needs of the heart can be supplied. We all begin by seeking people to meet these core needs. Unfortunately, long after we enter into a relationship with Jesus many of us continue to rely on others in family, school, work, marriage, and other personal relationships. Consequently, the typical believer neglects to passionately pursue the one relationship that has been designed and designated to include provision for these and so many other needs in their life.[18] This vital relationship with our heavenly Father simply cannot be developed without investing your love and significant time in His Presence, just one-on-one. Really, what intimate relationship can be healthy without a significant personal investment? Jesus died so that you could enter into a relationship with God, as your Father, but you are responsible for developing it, daily.[19]

Final Thoughts

Most of us are living a life with a hundred things distracting, entangling, and pulling us in different directions. This world is very much like quicksand, as we step into it, we begin to get sucked-down because of the nature and composition of this natural "trap". The moment we react to the downward pulling, we find that our own efforts only lead us deeper into the abyss. This world is just as deadly, if we become overwhelmed and consumed with the pressing issues of daily life. Survival experts say, "Quicksand sucks down and engulfs objects on contact" and "To cross over it, you must lay face down, spread your arms and legs, and move slowly"![1] It seems that we are often running through life flailing and kicking, seemingly to get ahead and move to the other side of circumstances or situations.

On the contrary, the Bible teaches us that if we lay prostrate, in humility, submission, and adoration (Biblical worship) before our Father and patiently wait on Him, as the all-sufficient One, then we will see His goodness and He will cause us to rest.[2] Wouldn't it be a great relief if you could rest in the midst of overwhelming circumstances and know that good success is guaranteed? Only when we are at rest, resulting from His peace and intimate knowledge of Him, though surrounded by things that lead to death, can we reverse the downward pull and rise to solid ground upon the Rock.[3]

If you are like most of us, then you really do want to hear God's voice and be directed by the Holy Spirit, but with all of the noise (i.e. 24-hour news,

Internet, digital music, instant messaging, podcasts, email, and millions of apps available on your phone) you can barely hear your own voice. You *can* learn to hear the still, small voice of our Father, even in the midst of the whirlwinds of life.[4]

Dear reader, will you join me in our Father's Presence where there is peace, promise, and provision? Are you ready to become like a little child, today?

Definitions

Spiritual Keys

Submission: Jesus, our Master Teacher, prayed the prayer of submission just before facing His final assignment.[1] In order to reach His divine destiny, He had to give Himself over to death and this proved to be His greatest challenge, personally.[2] He surrendered His will to the Father's will and received the provision (strength, faith, hope, etc.) needed to fulfill His destiny.[3] We must release our will to God, too, and submit to His will each day. If we choose to exalt our will over His, then we are guilty of idolatry. We cannot expect to benefit from this type of disjointed relationship. The root of sin is rebellion against God's authority and we understand that He cannot tolerate anyone or anything taking His rightful place in our lives.[4] Submission to His will establishes the proper relationship between you and our Father God. Submission requires faith that His will is perfect and the understanding that ours is not perfect.[5]

Obedience: We find in the life of Jesus that His complete obedience, even to death, was the key that reestablished the kingdom of God and His sovereign rule here on earth.[6] In the same way, our complete obedience, resulting from our love for Jesus as Savior and Lord and our personal relationship with our heavenly Father, is the key that establishes the kingdom of God in our hearts.[7] Unless I fully obey His general instructions in the Bible *and* His specific

53

instructions revealed by the Holy Spirit, I will never succeed at my unique assignment (individual purpose).[8] How can we obey each day, if we cannot recognize His voice? How can we recognize His voice, if we do not spend time with Him each day? We cannot! My inability to hear God's voice and obey His daily instructions because I invest limited time in His Presence must be counted as disobedience. Why? He gives you time and His Word, then you choose to invest time with Him or not. God cannot honor a life of disobedience because, simply put, "Disobedience is sin".[9] Please remember that delayed obedience is disobedience, as well. If this truth does not "fit" with your current perspective, just ask any parent how *they* view "delayed obedience". See beloved, as little children of God, we must learn to listen and obey, in faith.

Forgiveness: According to the Bible, forgiveness is not an optional, but a requirement.[10] It is a spiritual key that unlocks God's forgiveness for us. We understand that the level of God's forgiveness towards us, after salvation, is directly related to our willingness to forgive others.[11] It is true that we, with our own limited power, cannot forgive everyone for everything. This is why we need to spend time in our Father's Presence and become more aware of the depth and breadth of His forgiveness towards us. We are then empowered by this understanding, our personal experience of His mercy, and the Holy Spirit, to extend mercy and forgiveness to others.[12] According to His Word, He cannot forgive our sin of unforgiveness until we forgive others.

Terms

Assignment: Your individual purpose, which leads to your divine destiny, is your God-given assignment. There is a specific problem, which you were uniquely created to solve, that clarifies your eternal significance. Some people refer to it as your purpose or the answer to, "Why am I here?", but this is *not* the same as the general purposes revealed in the Bible, which have been widely written and preached about in recent years. Your Assignment can only be revealed and achieved in Father God's Presence.[13] Our Father created you with a unique set of natural skills, specific life experiences, and spiritual gifts, so you can address the problem/need that you have been assigned to solve.[14] True and eternal success (or significance) in your life is dependent upon your pursuit of God's assignment and your willingness to follow His daily instructions. What you love, what grieves you, and how you invest your time can provide clues to your assignment or individual purpose, but you cannot identify it by self-analysis or skill set inventory, alone. Most importantly, you cannot successfully complete your assignment without our Father's guidance and provision, mercy and grace.[15] In partnership with God, peace, promotion, and provision are found in your pursuit of this assignment, which is the will of God for *your* life.[16] If you want to reach your destiny, then you must know your assignment and live in His Presence.

Full-Life™ Wealth: Full-Life™ includes spiritual, physical, emotional, and financial aspects of life. Our Father wants you whole and complete in all aspects of the *one* life you have to live![17] Wealth is defined as abundance, acquisition, benefit, asset, advantage, supply, and/or reserve. Full-Life™ Wealth is the aggregate benefit of living as royalty, a joint-heir with Jesus.[18]

Endnotes

Introduction
1. Romans 8:16-17
2. Luke 5:8-10
3. Jeremiah 1:4-10
4. Romans 10:9-10
5. Luke 10:40-42, Matthew 6:34, 1 John 1:8-10

Chapter One
1. Mark 10:14-16
2. Luke 18:17
3. Matthew 18:4
4. Luke 18:14
5. Colossians 3:1-2

Chapter Two
1. Matthew 18:4
2. Matthew 6:34
3. James 1:6-8, Mark 11:24
4. Genesis 1, Isaiah 55:11, Luke 1:37
5. Luke 18:18-23
6. Matthew 6:19-21
7. 1 John 4:8, Lamentations 3:21-23
8. Jeremiah 29:11, Ephesians 2:10
9. Matthew 26:38-39 (AB)
10. Philippians 2:8-9
11. Matthew 6:10
12. 1 Corinthians 6:19-20, Matthew 25:14-30
13. Matthew 5:5,7,8, 18:4
14. Mark 11:25
15. Luke 18:1-8
16. Matthew 7:7

Chapter Three
1. Matthew 18:3
2. Luke 10:21

3. Matthew 22:37-40
4. Matthew 6:25-26
5. Luke 10:39, 42, Luke 22:69, Colossians 3:1-2
6. Luke 1:37, Isaiah 55:11
7. Genesis 3:8
8. Lamentations 3:21-23, 1 John 4:8
9. Hebrews 12:5-7
10. Isaiah 14:13-14
11. Proverbs 3:11-12
12. 1 Samuel 15:22
13. John 14:15
14. Hebrews 12:5-7
15. Deuteronomy 28
16. Proverbs 13:24, 22:6,15, 23:13, 29:15
17. John 3:16, Romans 8:12-17
18. Matthew 6:25-34
19. John 15:5

Chapter Four
1. John 13:2-5
2. Matthew 26:39
3. 2 Corinthians 5:17, Romans 8:16, 37, Galatians 3:13-14
4. Genesis 17:5 (AB)
5. 2 Corinthians 3:18, Exodus 34:29-35
6. Exodus 34-29
7. Romans 10:9, 8:16
8. Genesis 32:28, 35:10
9. Joshua 1:9
10. Psalm 91:1
11. Mark 13:7, Psalm 91:7
12. Luke 5:7, 10
13. John 12:3, 7, Mark 14:9
14. Jeremiah 29:11

15. Purpose Driven Life, book, R. Warren
16. Jeremiah 1:5, Ephesians 2:10
17. Ecclesiastes 10:10, Daniel 5:14, Luke 2:40
18. Matthew 6:25-34, Genesis 22:14
19. John 14:6, Matthew 11:28-31, Luke 9:23, Matthew 7:23

Final Thoughts
1. www.wilderness-survival.com
2. Genesis 17:1-8, 2 Corinthians 12:9, Psalm 27:13, Matthew 11:28 (AB)
3. John 14:27, 2 Samuel 22:47, Psalm 49:2, 71:1, 89:26, 95:1 Matthew 7:24-27
4. 1 Kings 19:11-15

Spiritual Keys & Definitions
1. Matthew 26:42
2. Matthew 26:38-39
3. John 18:11
4. Isaiah 14:12-15
5. Romans 12:2, 2 Samuel 22:31
6. Philippians 2:8
7. John 14:15, Luke 17:20-21
8. John 15:5
9. Genesis 2:16-17, Genesis 3:6-13
10. Matthew 18:20-24
11. Matthew 6:9-15
12. Lamentations 3:21-23
13. Isaiah 29:16, 64:8, John 15:5,8
14. Romans 11:29, Matthew 26:54
15. 2 Corinthians 12:9, John 15:5
16. 1 Corinthians 3:9
17. 3 John 1:2
18. Romans 8:17

About JD Nardone

JD Nardone founded Marketplace Renewal Int'l, in 2005, to equip Christians for Full-Life™ success. Full-Life™ includes spiritual, physical, emotional, and financial aspects of life (professional and personal). The vision for Marketplace Renewal Int'l was birthed from over twenty-seven months of weekly Bible study and prayer meetings held in both a Fortune 500 company and a private company with just over 100 employees. JD didn't focus on offering a workplace evangelism program, but rather a teaching program that helped people apply Biblical principles in their workplace, a prayer-group program that created a supportive workplace by focusing on specific needs throughout the company, and an individualized "coaching" program for executive management. On-site Chaplaincy services were offered in the company chapel and personal crisis counseling and visitation services were also provided. JD gained invaluable and life changing experience as he ministered to Christians and non-Christians, in the marketplace, five days per week.

He continues to coach senior executives and business owners, equip marketplace leaders, and write books that help Christians of all ages live by faith, so they can live supernaturally! After years of working with 100's of individuals, JD is convinced that every person can develop a Presence Driven™ Lifestyle.

Brother JD visits churches and groups as part of a prophetic commission to speak the Truth, "equip the saints for the work of ministry", and advance the Kingdom of God via "Greater Works".
He can be reached at www.presence-driven.com